American Independence

in

verse

Bradford Skow

Published by Pentameter Press
Cambridge, MA
pentameterpress.com

American Independence in Verse

ISBN 979-8-9996327-1-5 (paperback)
ISBN 979-8-9996327-0-8 (eBook)
Library of Congress Control Number: 2025920348

Cover art / illustrations: Elliot Skow
Publication managed by AuthorImprints.com

For my family

Table of Contents

Preface i

Prologue 1

Part 1: Taxation Without Representation 5

    Interlude 29

Part 2: Occupation and Massacre 33

    Interlude 51

Part 3: War and Independence 57

Coda 81

About the Author. 85

Preface

These poems tell the story of American Independence, through the radicals who fought for it, and the Crown officials who tried to stop it. Moderates, loyalists, and fellow travelers also have their say. Each poem is based on a real speech, letter, pamphlet, or declaration, sometimes hewing closely to the source, sometimes making good use of poetic license. Some of the poems take up abstract questions of freedom, authority, and legitimate government, but there are also reports of mob violence, and a city groaning under military occupation; don't worry, there will be blood. We begin in 1765, when the Stamp Act provoked cries of taxation without representation, and end in 1776, with the war just begun, the new nation facing a hopeful if uncertain future, and Washington's troops hearing, for the first time, the Declaration of Independence read aloud.

PROLOGUE

Join or Die

Benjamin Franklin, The Albany Congress, 1754

One government uniting us
Is surely worth all the fuss,
As pulling us together would
Advance our interests and our good.

In council meetings, reps would learn
Respect, and how to take their turn,
And forge through their deliberation
The people of a single nation.

If separate, all our enemies
Will violate our liberties
And conquer *one* while *twelve* stand by.
We thirteen states must *Join, or Die.*

But I well know that well-laid plans
Are seldom fetched from wisdom's hands.
Instead they wait on that event
They were intended to prevent.

PART 1:
Taxation Without Representation

The Administration of the Colonies

Thomas Pownall (former Governor of Massachusetts), London, 1764

One cannot help but see that something new
Is rising in the world, either to be
Guarded against, or turned to our advantage.
America has woken to her strength
And vague impressions of a coming crisis
Worry every face. My sentiments are these:
We must unite their interests to our own—
But keep the springs of power on this island.
Some suggest we handle them with care
Lest in some future time they separate;
But I know that revolt and independence
From this Great Britain cuts against their nature.
A mechanical affection for us moves them;
England is *home*. But still the fact remains,
They claim the common right of Englishmen
That laws be made upon them only with
Their own consent. So I suggest,
For the preservation of our Empire,
That we encourage rivalry and jealousies
Between them. Unity is dangerous.

"To keep us just as poor as is your pleasure"

Jared Ingersoll to Thomas Whately (Joint Secretary to the Treasury), New Haven, July 6, 1764

I write replying to your new proposals
For laying taxes on the colonies.
You say we ought to pay our own defense;
We say the same on this side of the water,
And if the King would fix the cost, and wait,
Then we would do our part. These dreadful rumors
Of looming taxes stoke our apprehension.
Such precedent, once set, gives you the power
To keep us just as poor as is your pleasure.
From this I leave to you to guess
How many strategies could be invented
To dodge a tax that's thought to violate
Our natural rights and liberties. Don't think
That I'm impertinent. I advocate
So much for your side of the water, that
My countrymen regard me with suspicion.
I've always been persuaded that a body
Respectable as England's Parliament
Would not do anything unjust or wrong.
I also know that any method which
Your fancy might suggest for taxing us
Would go down with my people like chopped hay.
On these points, you distrust our testimony;
I wish you'd see the more than equal danger
Of seemingly disinterested opinions.
I now await impatiently the ship
Which, God willing, takes me there to England.
I expect her in the hour.

"These Sons of Liberty will but grow stronger"

Debate in the House of Commons, February 6, 1765

I. The Government

Parliament's power to tax is just,
    and quite hard won.
If over them we have not this,
    then we have none.
And then America, with all her wealth
Becomes a kingdom to herself.

II. Charles Townshend

By our indulgence nourished
America has flourished.
Will they not grudge a tiny share
To help relieve the debt we bear?

III. Isaac Barré

Them planted by your care? No!
They fled your tyranny to hostile land,
Whose hardships were relief from what they suffered here.

Them nourished by indulgence? No!
They grew by your neglect.

Protected by your arms? No!
They took up arms in your defense,
And their frontier was drenched in blood.

Remember on this day my warning:
The spirit that first actuated
These *Sons of Liberty*
Will but grow stronger from this Act.

The Stamp Act

Parliament, March 22, 1765

Our colonies in America we
Defend; protect; secure;
And money for all these adventures
We pass this Act to procure.

Every skin or piece of parchment
Or vellum or paper or scrap
You use for the following purposes
On it a tax we now slap.

A warrant's a shilling or two, and
A deed for land is four;
A license for booze is three whole pounds
And stamps for dice cost more.

Of prices there are a great number
Depending on what you will write
And don't you dare try to avoid them
Or we'll pull your leashes tight.

The Virginia Resolves

Patrick Henry, House of Burgesses, Williamsburg, May 29, 1765

Whether through fear, or influence, this Act
Is met by other Colonies with silence.
Virginia then will be the first to speak.
I offer to this House these resolutions:
Resolved, the General Assembly of
This Colony maintains exclusive right
To lay a tax upon its own inhabitants.
Vesting that power in any other Person
Or Body will tend only to destroy
American as well as British freedom.
Resolved, Virginians are not bound to yield
Obedience to any law designed
To lay a tax upon them, if that law
Be not duly passed by this Assembly.
If anyone asserts the contrary,
He shall be deemed an enemy to this
Colony. *Caesar had his Brutus, and*
Charles had his Cromwell; and I do not doubt
That some American will soon stand up
In favor of this country.

Treason! Treason!

If this be treason—*make the most of it.*

"I am but governor in name"

Francis Bernard (Governor of Massachusetts) to the Board
of Trade in London, Castle William, Boston Harbor

August 15, 1765

My Lords,

I used to doubt that Boston would oppose
The Stamp Act. But Virginia's Resolutions
Have been a siren to the disaffected.
Every week, papers called for acts of opposition.
I did not think that they would start so soon,
Or go so far.

Yesterday was found, hanging from a tree,
An effigy of Andrew Oliver
With label reading: *In Praise of Liberty.*
He was to be the Stamp Act Officer.
I ordered that the Sheriff take it down,
But all his men refused; they said they feared
The danger to their lives. It then grew dark.
The Mob proceeded on to Oliver's shop,
Christened it the Stamp Office, and pulled it to
The ground. Next, to his house: the effigy
They there beheaded and then burned. They could
Not find the man himself, or else they surely
Would have murdered him. I called the Council,
Who said that the Militia would not act
Against the rioters. At sunset I
Escaped here, to the Castle. As I write
I see a bonfire burning on Fort Hill.

August 16

Oliver has today declared in public:
He will resign, and not act in the Office.
All say that the Stamp Act shall not be executed here;
And that a man who offers stamps shall be
Killed; and that all the power of Great Britain
Shall not oblige them to submit.

August 22

It is my opinion that the worst
Should be expected and provided for.
I am a prisoner-at-large;
Not ten men are here whom I command;
I am but Governor in name.

"Some American should draw his pen in her defense"

I. To his Friend in Rhode Island
Martin Howard, Halifax (Nova Scotia), January 20, 1765

I've no ambition to appear in print
But if these thoughts are worth the public eye
I leave you liberty to publish them.
With real concern I've watched the newspapers
Pouring abuse against the mother country;
It's time that some American should draw
His pen in her defense—nay, vindication.

The jurisdiction of our Parliament
Extends abroad to every English subject;
And that expansive Body represents,
In absentia, all their scattered interests.
While some suggest expanding membership,
I urge the danger of that innovation.
To mix in people from the far dominion
Would be unnatural, and destroy its symmetry.
Freedom and happiness will be secured
Not through a share of Parliamentary elections,
But though that Body's wisdom and its virtue.

I have but little malice in my heart
Yet idle moments find me wishing these
Unworthy sons of Britain could experience
The iron of the Spanish Inquisition.

II. To the People of Newport (Rhode Island)
Martin Howard, Newport Mercury, *August 26, 1765*

I too am native of these colonies,
My heart attached more warmly to their interests
Than the hearts of those who persecute me.
I've published my opinions with the freedom
That is the boast of every Englishman.
It's therefore with astonishment I see
My countrymen directing public fury
Against my person and my property.
Under the pretense that they serve the cause
Of freedom, they would take away the right
Of private judgment, and block up the avenues
Of truth. Indeed I only exercised
The very privilege that they claim and use
Against me. As for the positions I
Defended in my letter, I retract—none.

Declarations and Petitions of The Stamp Act Congress

New York City, October 1765

I. Declaration of Rights and Grievances

We write to offer humble thoughts upon
Our rights, and to convey our grievances
Against some recent Acts. We owe the same
Allegiance to the Crown, as any subject
Born in the realm. But their inherent *rights*
Are ours as well. We too are a free people.
Taxes need consent; but these colonies
Are not, and by their nature cannot be,
Represented in the House of Commons.
We thus with loyal duty ask you, please:
Repeal the Stamp Act; restore our liberties.

II. To the King's Most Excellent Majesty

We the people of your colonies
Devoted ever to your sacred Person
With warmest sentiments of love and duty
Beg permission to approach the throne.

First planted here by subjects of the Crown
In barren deserts and in barbarism
We built a flowering civilization
And spread humanity, and science, and knowledge.

And through the works and days of all our labor
A strong foundation laid on which your Empire
May yet become the largest and the greatest
Seen yet by history or by God above.

We ardently implore that you protect
The freedoms due to Englishmen by right.
If so, the riches you've received from us
Will pale beside the wealth you'll yet acquire.

Immense advantages have now been placed
In danger of forever being lost,
And we implore your Majesty's protection,
Convinced by proofs of your paternal love.

"I'm charged with giving birth to sedition in America"

Debate in the House of Commons, January 14, 1766

I. William Pitt

The rights of Englishmen protect America:
They are the sons, not the bastards, of England.
Some suggest that the Americans
Are virtually represented here;
I would fain know by whom. By you? Or some
Knight of the shire? This is the rotten part
Of our constitution, and if it
Does not wither on its own, we must
Suffer the knife that it be amputated.

II. George Grenville

Disturbances abroad have grown to tumults.
Indeed, they border on open rebellion,
And if the doctrines heard this day should be
Confirmed, they'll cross. Protection and obedience
Are reciprocal; America
Is bound to yield. But they renounce authority,
Insult our officers, while Gentlemen
Defend them, careless of the consequences.

III. William Pitt

I spoke my sentiments against this Act,
Freely; and now I'm charged with giving birth
To sedition in America.
And what have we become, when liberty
Of speech is called a crime in Parliament?
The gentleman tells us, America

Tilts toward rebellion; I rejoice to see
Resistance to oppression. And he inquires,
When were the colonies emancipated?
I desire to know when they were made slaves.
The Stamp Act is gross injustice.
I raise my hand against it. Will you punish
Americans for madness you have caused?
We who have acted wrong should be the first
To act with prudence. But do not stomp and frown;
I am no courtier of America.
I stand for Britain, and for Parliament's
Authority to bind and to restrain
The colonies. Our power over them
Is sovereign and supreme. The greater must
Rule the less. And if the cause be just,
Our boot may crush America to dust.

Benjamin Franklin in the
House of Commons

February 13, 1766

Affection and respect—obedience and
Submission freely given were, till now,
The temper of America toward Britain.
It cost no armies manning garrisons;
No nervous frowning redcoats stood to keep
That fruitful people subject to the Crown.
Just a few warm words penned in ink and paper.
There was a fondness for your laws and for
Your customs; for your fashions and your manners.
But now you dare impose on us this tax
When no one present represents our interest.
Here! In this Parliament we venerated:
This long-great bulwark of rights and freedom.
It is against the nature of the English
Constitution. We will not submit.
If you persist in this Act, and deny
Us commerce; and that we shall neither marry,
Nor make our wills, but you extort our money,
Or ruin us by the consequences of
Refusal...go, send out your arms and men,
You will not find rebellion. You may indeed make one.

"No more than the inhabitants of the moon"

"Britannus Americanus" (Samuel Adams),
Boston Gazette, *March 17, 1766*

The first settlers of this country
Were returned into the state of nature
Or else remained still subjects of the King.

If the first, then they reclaimed their natural rights,
And no power had authority to molest them
In their free enjoyment of those rights:
The Crown, or the people of Great Britain
No more than the inhabitants of the moon.

So by right they could design their government
    As they thought best.
As it happened, the people of New England
    Chose the King of Old England
    For their King.
But over them the *men* of England had no jurisdiction—
As they had none over men of Hanover,
Who were also subjects of their King;
Nor did any Body chosen by those men.
The settlers' covenant was with the King alone:
To him alone did they submit,
Under terms set down in royal charter.

On the second supposition, the settlers remained
Always subjects of the King.
They thus retained the English right
To consent to any law that binds them,
A right enjoyed by others who
Were no more than their equals.
Separated from England by rough seas,
To secure this right they founded and they authorized
Houses and Assemblies of their own.

We therefore may conclude:
For Parliament to tax America
Is no more equitable
Nor more consistent with the British constitution
Than for the Assemblies in this New England
To pluck the pockets under the name of "tax"
Of our fellow subjects in Great Britain.

Repeal of the Stamp Act;
The Declaratory Act

Parliament, March 18, 1766

We passed an Act of late
'Cause protecting you is expensive.
Developments since then
Have made us apprehensive.

Stamp Act enforcement
Is very inconvenient.
Second thoughts suggest
It's better to be lenient.

So:
May it please the King,
His Majesty most high,
That Act is null and void;
You do not need comply.

*

But don't get too excited.
We noticed that you broke
Our laws with resolutions
Throwing off our yoke.

So we Declare today
That you are and ought to be
Subordinate unto
The Crown of this Great-B.

And Parliament shall have
The power and the force
To bind you to this nation
In every case–of course.

So:
May it please the King,
His Majesty most high,
Your Acts are null and void
Before this ink is dry.

The Snare Broken

Jonathan Mayhew, Sermon at West Church (Boston), May 23, 1766

The snare is broken, our souls are freed;
Our help is in the Lord, who made both earth and heaven.

We have known drought, and pestilence, and death.
And we have known war: French and savage armies
Destroyed our homes and tore our lands. But never
Have we known a time of such anxiety
As came when Parliament approved that Act
Which threatened us with abject slavery.
Together we resolved a desperate plan
To run all risks, and to tempt every hazard,
Preferring death itself to an inglorious
Servitude. We owe thanks to God, whose hands
Cradle the hearts of men, as into us
He breathed a spirit of liberty. He has
Given us beauty for ash, and has turned
Our groans to songs. I will not meddle with
The thorny question whether, and so when,
Subjects may seize the reins of government;
But I do say that in some form, this right
Cannot be denied. To close I pray:
Almighty Lord, if any in the world
Be driven out, and seek a safe retreat
From slavery, let them find, O let them find
A home here under thy soft, brooding wings.
Amen.

"The motive for repeal was prudence, not principle"

Silas Downer to the New York Sons of Liberty, Providence, July 21, 1766

I write returning your congratulations
On the Stamp Act repeal. But vigilance
Is needed now as much as was before.
The motive for repeal was prudence, not
Principle. Note their strange resolves, that pave
A way for taxes to be laid again.
Petitions from the colonies were met
Only with wrath, and indignation, and
Contempt. And my hands shake when I reflect
That some commoner, representing half
A score of beggars in some English shithole
Town, should talk big about securing our
"Dependence on the mother country," when
He only means himself. I have seen others
Express their thanks, and bow and lick the dust,
And ask their pardon of the woolen-drapers
And the nail-makers for our "disobedience";
I turned away disgusted. To those men
Chosen by people of another realm
Whose only merit was to un-make an
Act which they had no right to make, we owe
Nothing. Their declarations, newly made,
Of love and tenderness, are only meant
To lull us into sleep, the better to
Execute plans for total subjugation
To the despotic will of Parliament.
Many are here, who for a shilling would
Surrender the whole freedom of this country—
But for the Sons of Liberty, who have
With firm and steady hands turned them aright.

Much work remains to do, while the days last,
And I will die before I yield my freedom.

"A lurking serpent lies concealed"

Samuel Adams to Christopher Gadsden, Boston, December 11, 1766

My good friend Otis mentions you
    With great respect,
Having sat with you of late in Congress;
He says that you were zealous in the Cause.
What a blessing has the Stamp Act proved,
Though calculated to enslave and ruin us.
The friendships and connections made in opposition
Shall deter the enemy from making
New attempts upon our rights.
Yet a lurking serpent lies concealed,
And if unnoticed by a wary passenger,
Will dart its fatal venom.

Interlude

"There were a few who hankered after independence"

I. George Washington to Robert McKenzie,
Philadelphia, October 9, 1774

I find I must be candid, and confess
That your opinions have been led astray
By venal men, who falsely counsel you
That Massachusetts is rebellious,
And that it aims for independency.
Give me leave, my good friend, to say to you,
You are abused. I am as satisfied,
As I am of my own existence, that
No such thing is intended or desired,
By any thinking man in North America.

II. From *The History of the Rise, Progress, and Establishment, of the Independence of the United States of America*, William Gordon, 1788

Even most Patriots preferred to see
Harmonious relations soon restored;
All memory of recent animosity
Obliterated; and a return to life
Secure in the warm shadow of the mother country.
But there were a few who hankered after
Independence: behind their printed masks
To this they bent their will entire.

III. John Adams to Benjamin Rush, Quincy
(Massachusetts), May 21, 1807

Two years before the Declaration, cold and wet,
I stepped into a tavern outside Boston.
Drying my coat beside the bar-room fire,
I heard one say, "The people of the town

Are much distracted." Another answered him,
"Oppression will make wise men mad." They argued
Politics for some time, before a third
Injected: *it's high time that we rebel.*
That's why, you see, I've always laughed when men
Assert that independence was a late
Invention. That potential remedy,
Should Britain overreach, has lived in us
Ever since the Puritans arrived.
But in our generation there was one
Who was the first to raise the thought, and to
Secret it in the people's hearts for later harvest.

PART 2:

Occupation and Massacre

Letters from a Farmer in Pennsylvania

John Dickinson, Philadelphia, 1767–68

My Dear Countrymen:
New duties have been laid on certain goods
We're bound by law to buy from England: glass,
Paper, lead, paint, and tea. It's said they're not
Internal taxes, and that Parliament,
Therefore, has acted in its right. Not so:
A duty laid for revenue is tax;
If it be laid on us, then we are taxed;
If taxed without consent, then we are slaves.
Rouse yourselves at once, my dear countrymen:
Behold the ruin hanging over your heads.
Admit these duties, and the tragedy
Of our American liberty is finished.
Complying with this Act will warrant Britain,
Through precedent, to later evil use
Of falsely claimed authority.
And it will prove you tame, and if you bend
Your neck and take this yoke, they will not fear
To offer further bondage as they please.
Like a bird sent across the sea to tell
Whether the violent waves that agitated
Distant waters have yet stilled, this Act
Is an *experiment upon your disposition.*
What striving power seizes, it will keep.

But our resistance must be that of dutiful
Children, who have received unmerited
Blows from a much-loved parent. Our complaints
Must speak the quiet tones of veneration.
With calm resolve, the proper road remains
To assemble and petition for relief.
Differences, unattended, grow to anger;

Imprudent acts create incurable
Rage. And what then? If once we're separated
From the mother country, torn from her
To whom we're bound by laws and warm affection—
We must bleed at every vein.

"The time has come to show our strengthened hand"

The Earl of Hillsborough (Secretary of State for the Colonies) to Governor Bernard, Whitehall (London), July 30, 1768

The King commands me tell you that our troops
Immediately will be sent and landed
In Boston. For too long has it resisted
The laws and the authority of Parliament.
The time has come to show our strengthened hand;
His Majesty, now moved to interpose
His great authority, will thus induce
Obedience to the law. Yet you alone
Must stand responsible for making peace.
Remiss of duty will not be excused;
And pleas of danger in official acts
Will sound as hollow pretense. We do advise
Removing from their office all such persons
As are infected with an opposition
To Parliament's just power. While Boston is
Possessed by a licentious, unrestrained
Mob, Colonial government cannot
Proceed. It is the King's benevolent wish
That by lenient methods Boston learn
That those false doctrines and dangerous principles
Inculcated with diligence and art
By wicked men will lead to anarchy
And the subversion of our constitution,
And the destruction of the British Empire.

"The people of this province are uneasy"

"Determinatus" (Samuel Adams), Boston Gazette, *August 8, 1768*

That the people of this province are uneasy, all must allow.
That the people are disposed to mobbish violence, I utterly deny.

Some point to recent stirrings in the town:
But note well the circumstances.
When property is seized, under pretense of law,
 And by aid of military power;
When such violent acts excite resentment
 Even in the better sort of people
Can anyone be surprised?

And what was then the mighty consequence?
It may have been: some few persons did resent it.
It may have been: some few persons broke some panes of glass,
 And then dispersed in quiet calm.

The people of this province are enlightened:
They know the proper execution of the law
From the exercise of new, invented, and unconstitutional powers—
Powers repugnant to the British constitution
And the charter of this province.

I am no friend to riots, tumults, and unlawful assemblies.
But when the people are oppressed, their rights
Infringed, and their property invaded;
 When taskmasters are set above them;
 When ships with cannon execute unlawful acts
  Before their eyes;
 When royal governors dissolve their legislatures,
 Sweeping aside the delegates they empowered
  To guard their rights;
In such circumstances, the people will be discontented,
 And they should not be blamed.

In such circumstances, the people will assert their freedom boldly,
    While they have the spirit of freedom,
And they will be justified.

To whisper a complaint is called by some a riotous spirit.
But the people will complain, as is their right,
Until their grievances are redressed,
Lest they become fit only to be slaves
Of the dirty tools of arbitrary power.

The Journal of Occurrences

Various Newspapers, 1768–69

We now behold a town at perfect peace
With angry warships anchored in its harbor.

Troops occupy the courthouse, and defile
That seat of justice; they encamp on Boston Common.

The people are uneasy at the sight
Of soldiers harshly whipped for drunkenness.

The quartered troops are wretchedly debauched
And their licentiousness increases daily.

Peaceful inhabitants are stabbed and beaten
With muskets and with sharpened bayonets.

With promises of freedom, officers
Are urging slaves to cut their masters' throats.

Last night a soldier seized a married woman
By the neck, and threw her on the ground.

Another woman, screaming out in fear,
Was wounded by a knife run through her cheek.

An inquest judged a woman had been ravished
By soldiers, and had died while she resisted.

Guards warned a youth that if he did not answer,
They would immediately blow his brains out.

Merchants importing goods from Britain, to gratify
Their avaricious cravings, disadvantage
The cause of liberty. Let them be looked
Upon by all with eyes of sharp contempt.

Why do desertions grow? The troops have seen
The people here are cheerful, hearty, and well-clad;

And concluded that, although not rich,
This is the Promised Land, flowing with milk and honey.

The tighter this unconstitutional
Cable of power is drawn, the firmer we become;
Until the hand that's strong enough to break us
Must break the pillars of the British constitution.

Some now assert, of loyal subjects arming
Themselves, within the law, that we intend
To cause an insurrection. But if the secrets
Of the human breast be so transparent,
We may as easily affirm that they
In calling for a military force
Intend to introduce a general massacre.

"If the Devil were himself their scribe"

Governor Bernard to the Earl of Hillsborough,
Boston, February 25, 1769

My Lord,

I've here included several issues of
The *Boston Evening Post*, where Samuel Adams,
With his assistants, constantly perverts,
Misrepresents and falsifies what's said
And done in Council. If the Devil were
Himself their scribe, he could not have produced
A greater package of seditious lies.
They publish at torrential rate; the few
Pens I have cannot answer. Adams has contrived
To circulate these lies across the colonies,
To raise a general clamor against our
Government. A report from me will follow
About the troops' behavior, proving false
Accounts that have been printed. Never have
So many troops, while quartered in a town
Licentious as is Boston, exhibited
Such patience; even as the townsmen are
With every act provoking them to violence.

"The consequence arising from our independence"

"Alfred" (Samuel Adams), Boston Gazette, *October 2, 1769*

Let us take a retrospect
Of American affairs.
Determined opposition to the Stamp Act
Operated its repeal.
But that detestable legislation
Created jealousies that still abide,
And in the whole may not subside—
Jealousies that may well be
The ruin of a glorious empire;
And may accelerate the consequence
Arising from our independence
Which
Whenever it may happen,
Will be fatal to the British kingdom;
For Britain is a haughty nation drunk with power
And acts the drunken man upon a precipice.

Of late a cursed cabal residing in this town
Intrigued to bring about another tax
Intending they to feast and fatten on
The spoils and plunder of the people.
They thought the colonies were reconciled.
But now,
They see the truth with grief and with despair, and
They soon will see with terror and amazement:
The colonies, united in determined opposition,
Will resist until the locusts and the caterpillars
That buzz and swarm among us
Are driven off into the wind like chaff.

The Deposition of Captain Molesworth

Sworn in Boston, November 3, 1769

Outside my window Ensign Ness was marching
The Neck Guard to the barracks, followed by a mob.
The crowd began to press against the soldiers;
A blacksmith struck one soldier such a blow
That blood flowed freely from his nose and mouth.
At this, four of the guard fixed bayonets.
By then I'd joined. I took command, and ordered
That none should strike the mob, unless obliged
In self-defense—"but if a man strikes you,
"Then you may run him through." At this
The crowd held back, and the guard marched
Into the barracks. In resentment of
My order, the blacksmith swore *if there be law*
In Boston, I will be revenged. A warrant
Signed, I was apprehended, and in court
Examined with some other officers
By Justice Dana. "Who brought you here? Who sent for you?"
He shouted. "By what authority do you
Mount guard, or march with arms?" And then to me:
"What was your aim? Emboldening your men
To murder the inhabitants? There's no
Walking the streets, nor day nor night, for hourly
Are gross abuses perpetrated by
Your soldiers. If a townsman should have struck
Any of you, even with fist or stick,
And you returned the blow and killed him dead,
Well then by God you would have swung for it."

"I'd rather be a slave to one master"

Theophilus Lillie, Boston Chronicle, *January 15, 1770*

The papers print that I "audaciously" import,
"Against united sentiment," British goods.
Now I've not entered far into the mysteries
Of government. I mind my business, and my shop.
But always it's seemed strange to me, that people
Who contend so much for civil liberty
Should be so ready to employ coercion;
That men who protest laws laid upon them
Without consent should dare to execute
On me their laws, to which I certainly
Have not agreed. I own I'd rather be
A slave to one master whom I might learn to please,
Than a slave to hundreds whom I cannot find.

A Short Narrative of the Horrid Massacre in Boston

Printed by Order of the Town of Boston, March 1770

Soldiers marauding through the town, and quarreling
With the inhabitants, occasioned men
To ring the meeting-house bell. Some lads gathered
Around the sentry at the Custom House.
Foul language was exchanged, and insults hurled;
The sentry stepped up and demanded that
One of the boys should show his face. The lad
Replied, *I'm not ashamed to show my face*
To any man. At this the sentry swung
His musket, smashing the boy's head; the boy
Staggered and bled. It was then Captain Preston
Issued from the Guard House with his soldiers.
They pushed the crowd with bayonets, so rough
As if intent on causing a disturbance.
They posted half a circle round the sentry.
The people, throwing snowballs, yelled and jeered.
At this the Captain gave the order: *Fire!–*
Damn you, fire, be the consequences what they will!
This fatal act left three men dead, and more
Struggling for life.

The Case of Captain Preston

Captain Thomas Preston, Boston Jail, March 12, 1770

Monday near Eight, two soldiers were attacked.
Alarm bells rang, a mob assembled, and,
Descending on the Custom House, surrounded
The sentinel, poised to execute its vengeance.
I ordered seven men to his protection.
The mob increased, and struck their clubs together,
And called, *you bloody backs, you Lobster scoundrels,*
Fire if you dare, fire and be damned! I parleyed,
Endeavoring with all my power that they
Retire in peace—to no avail. They pushed,
And pressed themselves against our bayonets.
One bystander asked if the guns were charged;
I replied yes, but that I had no mind
To order "fire"; indeed I stood before
The muzzles, and must fall a sacrifice
If any did. As I was speaking, one
Soldier received a blow, and stepped aside,
And instantly he fired. I turned to reprimand;
A club fell on my arm—which blow, had it
Landed upon my head, would mean my death.
The mob then launched a general attack;
Several soldiers fired in turn; which made
The mob disperse, save three unhappy men
Who instantly expired. Now malcontents,
Using every method, fish for evidence
To prove a plot to murder the inhabitants.
Others are infusing malice and revenge
Into the minds of those who'll be my jurors,
With false reports and other artifices.
So I, though innocent, am left with nothing
To expect but ignominious loss of life.

"Nature held him with an upright dignity"

John Adams to William Tudor, Quincy, April 15, 1818

A worthy painting of the scene would need
The greatest master's greatest art. Up front,
The council seated, Hutchinson presiding,
Costumed in white wigs and bright scarlet cloaks.
Petitioning for the inhabitants
Was Samuel Adams, dressed in plain simplicity.
Thucydides would write a speech for him;
That is beyond my powers. He represented
The public's justified determination
That all the troops be taken from the town:
Recent events had proved the ruinous
Effects of standing armies. He held himself,
Or rather Nature held him, with an upright
Dignity of figure and of gesture.
This was a delicate and dangerous crisis.
No redcoat's life was safe in any street
In town; the lives of the inhabitants
No more secure. Even I took my shift
To guard against a breach of peace. The governor,
Conferring with the colonel, hazarded
That they could send one regiment away,
If that would satisfy the people. At this,
Samuel arose, and he stretched forth his arm,
Even then quivering with palsy, saying,
If one could be removed, then so could two;
And nothing short of a complete evacuation
By all the troops could yet restore the peace,
Or satisfy the public mind. With that,
Boston was free.

"Some persons must have been at fault"

"Vindex" (Samuel Adams), Boston Gazette, *January 21, 1771*

As the lives of five of his Majesty's subjects
Were unfairly lost on the night of March 5th the last,
It follows that some persons must have been at fault.
Not the unhappy sufferers—they were in the peace
of God and King; let their memories
Remain unreproached.
It appears by the evidence in court
That all the prisoners were present in King Street;
That all discharged their muskets;
And that the men who died owed their deaths to musket balls.
Yet of the prisoners six were acquitted,
And two found guilty of manslaughter.
But I do not write in order to arraign the jurors
Before the bar of public opinion.
They are accountable to God
And to their own consciences;
And in *their* day of trial
May God send them good deliverance.

An Oration Commemorating
the Boston Massacre

Dr. Joseph Warren, Boston, March 5, 1772

People of Boston, and America:
That fatal fifth of March, now two years past,
Will never be forgotten—when our streets
Were stained with blood, and when the very air
Wept with the dying groans of slaughtered men.
Remember, always, how this came to be.
A standing army was established here
In time of peace, to enforce upon our shores
Obedience to Acts which any honest man
Would deem unjust. Soldiers ever are
The ready engines of oppression and
Of tyranny; this was the Crown's avowed
Design. Their unprovoked attack upon
Our slumbering innocents has gone unpunished—
But we who crossed a boisterous ocean to
Prepare the new world as a happy home
Of liberty, will not allow our grand
Experiment to die in vain. I say
To you my brothers, the self-same almighty
God who made bare his arm to save your fathers
Now watches over you with sword in hand,
And to the King across the sea I say
That we who late possessed the charms of freedom
Had rather die than see her torn from our embrace.

Interlude

"Everywhere, the spirit of equality prevails"

Henry Hulton (Commissioner of Customs) to Robert
Nicholson in Liverpool, Boston, August 3, 1771

In early spring I journeyed with my wife
Throughout this Province, and became convinced
That nothing less than the enthusiasm
And violent spirit of independency
That animated the first settlers
Could move a people to the arduous
Subduing of these lands to cultivation.
Although this land will never make them rich
Yet they increase wonderfully; and everywhere
The spirit of equality prevails.
Regarding social differences, they've no
Notion of rank, and will show more respect
To one another than to those above them.
They'll ask a thousand strange impertinent
Questions, sit down when they should wait at table,
React with puzzlement when you do not
Invite your valet to come share your meal.
I met few who may be called Gentlemen—
Few men of property, and education,
And liberal mind. I guess that when the first
Arrived, they built a shed, and ate salt pork,
And their descendants have not got much further.
A traveler finds no fresh provisions; he
Must drink their sour cider and New England
Rum. They feel no oppression from above,
See nothing to excite their envy or
Raise admiration, and what is human nature
If passions such as these are not aroused?
They take up lands without authority,
Live without law, or government; nor priest,

Nor magistrate; and with the least disturbance
Will easily tip into an insurrection.

Political Speculations

John Mein (loyalist publisher), Boston, 1774

The Puritans who birthed these people
Fled from England seeking freedom.
Yet in the colony they built
Dissidents were hanged or banished.

If you know them from their threats
Boston seems a teeming power.
But count their citizens and slaves:
They number scarcely fifteen thousand.

Slaves, indeed; for though they claim
A natural right to freedom which
Justifies—they say—rebellion;
They hold in bondage some two thousand souls.

PART 3:
War and Independence

The Committees of Correspondence

I. Letter to the Towns of Massachusetts
Boston Committee of Correspondence, November 20, 1772

We grow alarmed to see despotic plans
Pursued with vigor by our enemies.
Consulting with our brethren all throughout
The province, and the wider land, will prove
A wise and needed course. Thus, these committees
May exchange oppressions under which they groan.
Our wisdom cannot suffer us to doze,
Or sit supine, indifferent on the brink
Of our destruction, while an iron hand
Gorges daily on the choicest fruit
Stolen from that fair tree of Liberty
Our predecessors nourished with their blood.

II. To the Inhabitants of Massachusetts
"Massachusettensis" (David Leonard),
Massachusetts Gazette, *January 2, 1775*

These new Committees are as venomous
A serpent, as has ever issued from
The eggs of foul sedition. They erect
Themselves into tribunals, and play the role,
As one, of lawyer, witness, judge, and juror.
When widely scattered towns, in synchrony,
Erupt in turbulent distemper, they are
The secret conduits of the infection.
They've driven many from their homes
To seek protection from the British troops:
Sons, separated from their fathers; brothers
From their brothers; man and wife asunder.
In persecuting us they prove, that we

Are not unanimous. Their actions breed
Resentment. In this always-changing world,
It is wise to anticipate what will
Transpire, when the rolling wheel of time,
Ere long, should bring us to the uppermost.

"The die is cast"

December 17, 1773

I. The Diary of John Adams

There is a dignity, a majesty,
In this last effort of the Patriots.
So bold is this destruction of the tea,
So daring and intrepid, it will long
Stand one of history's epochal events.
As to the question of necessity:
To let the tea be landed, would concede
Ten years of labor, and subject ourselves,
And our posterity, forever to
Egyptian Taskmasters; and to contempt,
Reproach, oppression, even desolation.

II. John Adams to James Warren

The die is cast; the river has been passed,
And we have cut the bridge; this grand event
Surpasses any since the contest opened!
I'm charmed by its sublimity. The threats
And phantoms by the million, which shall be spread,
Are all imaginations. Yet even if
They should become realities, it were
Better that they be suffered, than to yield
And see the final ruin of our constitution.

The Intolerable Acts

Parliament, March, May, June, 1774

We're kind of mad
You dumped the tea.
Since you've been bad
We now decree:

1.
Boston's closed
To ship and boat,
To barge and hoy
And things that float.

2.
The charter signed
By Bill and M.
We now revoke
And condemn.

The King will now
Pick who's in charge;
And no town meetings
Small or large.

3.
If a King's man's charged
With a crime
We won't trust
Your courts this time.

He'll board a ship
And sail a mile
Returning here
For his trial.

4.
Last, not least
Our soldiers there
Need a place
To take the air.

In your spare beds
They now will lay
And don't expect
Us to pay.

"Nobody will be argued into slavery"

Edmund Burke, Speech on American Taxation,
Parliament, April 19, 1774

As we unleash our fearsome rights, to mark
The limits of their liberty, so they
Remove the muzzles from their own, to guard
Against the reach of our authority.
But all negotiations of the bounds
Of monsters, will destroy what they protect.
Leave the colonies to tax themselves;
Return to the old settlement. Respect
For safe tradition, is the argument
Of states and kings. Remand to the scholastics
This scrabbling over metaphysical
Distinctions, and all feuds will die away.
For if, unwisely, you sophisticate
And poison our authority with subtle
Deductions, from the boundless nature of
Our power, to consequences odious
To those you govern, all you'll teach them is
To call our right to rule in question. When
You drive him hard, the boar will surely turn
Upon the hunters. If our authority
Threaten their freedom, which will they fight for?
Nobody will be argued into slavery.

The Continental Congress

I. The Diary of John Adams,
June 20–25, 1774

The wisest men upon the continent
Are gathering to assemble in a Congress.
I feel myself unequal to the task.
A more extensive knowledge of the realm,
More expertise in law and policy,
Than I possess, is needed. And the thoughts,
Of all the people we now represent,
Are various as the faces that they wear.
I fear we have not men fit for these times.

II. John Adams to James Warren,
June 25, 1774

It will be—the Court of Areopagus,
The Council of Amphictyons, or perhaps
A conclave, or a Sanhedrin. Who knows.
A nursery of American political
Prophets. I hope it thrives. One ugly scene
Returns to me repeatedly in dreams:
Brutus and Cassius are defeated, and then slain.

A Summary View of the Rights
of British America

Intended for the Inspection of Virginia's Delegates to Congress
Thomas Jefferson, Williamsburg, July 1774

When Saxons left the European wilds
And settled England, they acted on a right,
That nature gave to all, to leave a country
Where chance, not choice, had placed them, and to make
Societies and laws in a new land.
And so our ancestors sailed to America.
Their blood was spilt to get the land to farm;
Their fortunes spent to cultivate the land.
For themselves they fought, and what they won
Is theirs by right to hold. Thus, Parliament
Has no authority here. A few Britons
Cannot give laws to millions in America
Who equal them in wisdom and in strength.
A slave's a slave though he serves many masters.

If we here boldly speak our grievances,
We speak as free men enjoying rights
Derived from nature, not the gift of kings.
Let those flatter who fear.

The Suffolk Resolves

Convention of the Committees of Correspondence,
Milton (Massachusetts), September 9, 1774

The fate of this New World waits now on us,
To make and to transmit to our posterity
A great inheritance unclogged by shackles.
This boundless continent, inhabited
By countless millions, will not submit to live
And have its being at the arbitrary
Will of a licentious minister.
Therefore we resolve, that no obedience
Is due to recent Acts, whose aim is to
Enslave America; and that our enemies,
Flattering themselves that they shall make of us
An easy prey, will learn instead how well
We are acquainted with the art of war.

A Candid Examination of the Mutual Claims of Great Britain and the Colonies

Joseph Galloway (former delegate to Congress), New York, 1775

This Congress has produced, in two months' labor,
Only a deformed and diminutive
Brat, INDEPENDENCY; and has prevailed
Upon the people to adopt this spurious
Infant, and take up arms in its defense.
They rush you to a black rebellion, and
Palpable treason. Meanwhile, they prepare
The rods and scourges of *their* tyranny
In order to subdue you. The authority
Of government is silenced by the din
Of war. These men, who have assumed the robes
Of guardians, will plunge you to your death,
Unless you now, with all the fortitude
Which virtue and which reason can inspire,
Oppose their horrible designs. Should they
Succeed, we soon will be a prey to foreign
Powers, our manners changed for arbitrary
Customs, and our religion will become
The bloody superstition of the Roman Pope.
And if we should escape that fate, we'll burn
In civil strife amongst ourselves; and their
Vaulting ambition will supply the fuel.

Taxation No Tyranny

Samuel Johnson, London, March 1775

I.
We are told that the Americans
Fled tyranny to rocks and desert lands,
Worked hard for crusts of bread, and suffer now
Invasion, and theft of all property,
By the harpies of taxation. But as this tale
Begins to melt our hearts in tearful pity,
Another advocate, aiming to raise
Our veneration, extols the fertility
Of their land, and the splendor of their towns;
An opulence suggesting our restrictions
Are light, and easily borne. The next reply
Informs us, that they descend from men who left
Everything to secure their liberty;
Too obstinate to be persuaded, and
Too powerful to be constrained; that they
Number three million, not merely men, but Whigs,
And that they multiply like rattlesnakes.
But if they shoot up like the Hydra, we do well
To consider how the Hydra was destroyed.

II.
A colony is to the mother country
As member to the body; and receives
From her the benefits and evils both
Of health and of disease. It's liable,
In dangerous maladies, to drastic treatments;
So if it be incurably infected,
Amputation may become the only course.

III.

He that enjoys the brightness of the sunshine
Must quit the coolness of the shade. Just so,
He who by choice departed for America
Cannot complain of losing what remains
In England. Once he had the right to vote;
It's he who made its exercise impossible.
He by his own consent has thrown his interest
Into the general mass, exchanging it
For that which he perceived to be his greater good.

IV.

That our revenge will touch the innocent,
Without redress, is much to be lamented;
But the guilt of rebellion aggregates to all.

V.

Those unable to display Americans
In any form that causes love, or pity,
Dress them in the habiliments of terror,
And crown them undefeatable; we're told
That should their towns fall under our control,
We'll only find abandoned houses; they
Will melt into the country, and bide their time.
But that's no reason to resign what's ours.
What foolishness to jump into the sea
In order to escape a leaky ship.

VI.

It's said that the subjection of America
Will but diminish our own liberties.
But if slavery be so fatally contagious,
Why are the loudest yelps for freedom heard
From gentlemen who, at their haughty leisure,
Buy and sell their fellow man?

VII.

It is my wish that this commotion end
Through terror, not through violence; that we subdue
Through use of dominating force, which shall
Destroy both the power and hope of all resistance.

Lexington and Concord

I. Paul Revere, Memorandum on Events of April 18, 1775

I was sent for by Doctor Joseph Warren,
The night of 18 April. He desired
I go to Lexington, and there inform
Adams and Hancock, that light troops and grenadiers
Were marching to the bottom of the Common,
Where boats were waiting; aiming, it was thought,
For Lexington, to take them prisoner
Or else destroy colonial stores in Concord.
I left at once, and crossed the Charles; in town,
Acquired a horse, and rode. The moon shone bright.
I sounded the alarm, then joined with Dawes,
When British officers accosted me.
They shouted, "God damn you—stop! One more inch
And you're a dead man." Pistol to my breast,
They ordered I dismount, and were surprised
To learn how early I had left from Boston.
But still the officers were confident.
I said they'd miss their aim: I knew what they
Were after, and I'd alarmed the countryside,
And I should have five hundred men there soon.
One of them clapped his pistol to my head:
"Tell the truth, or I will blow your brains out!"
I told him I esteemed myself a man of truth,
And that by what right he took me prisoner
I knew not; and that I was not afraid.

II. The Diary of Lieutenant Frederick MacKenzie,
Royal Welsh Fusiliers

When we arrived in Lexington, the infantry
Were in retreat from Rebel fire. The Rebels,
Considerable in number, lay concealed
And scattered behind fences and stone walls.
From there they fired on us in perfect safety.
The troops returned the fire, but with too much
Eagerness; most of it was thrown away.
It was resolved that we return to Boston.
Several troops were killed by unseen fire,
Which so enraged the soldiers that they forced
Open suspicious houses, and all they found
They put to death. Despite clear orders, some
Houses were plundered, and plundering soldiers killed,
Ambushed from cellars and dark nooks. Returned
To Barracks, we were ordered to sleep dressed.
The town is now besieged by Rebel arms.

Address to the Continental Congress

George Washington, Philadelphia, June 16, 1775

You do me a high honor. Yet I must
Admit a great distress at this appointment:
I cannot help but fear that all my strength,
And all my time in arms, may not be equal
To this extensive trust. But I will stand.
With cordial gratitude for praise received,
I bid goodbye to my domestic ease
And take up now my sword, and in your service
Will exert all power possessed in me
To prosecute This Glorious Cause.

"We're stuck between the hawk and buzzard"

I. The Olive Branch Petition, Congress,
Philadelphia, July 5, 1775

Most Gracious Sovereign:
We your faithful subjects, representing
In General Congress your American
Colonies, with humility entreat
Your Highness to attend to our petition.
The wealth and strength produced by the great union
Of colony, and mother country, under your
Just and mild government, became in time
The wonder of the world. That wonder bred
Envy, and brought war. Side by side we fought
To victory, and we in valor won
Your Majesty's own approbation. Thus
The pain, alarm, and the astonishment
We felt at the adoption of new rules
For our administration. We decline
Here the ungrateful task of drawing out
The irksome artifices, and delusive
Pretenses, practiced by your Ministers
In their attempts to execute these laws.
Your agents' violent enforcement has
Compelled us now to arm in our defense.
These civil discords may create incurable
Animosities. Our duty to
Almighty God, therefore, calls us to use
All measures to avert this crisis that
Remain compatible with our own safety.
We aim to execute this office with
The utmost deference to your Majesty;
Fondly we cling to your great Person, with

All possible devotion and affection;
And ardently desire our former harmony.
Therefore, we now beseech Your Majesty:
Interpose your authority, procure
For us relief from these disorders, and
With your wise acts create a long-enduring
Reconciliation. That your Great
Majesty's reign be long and prosperous
Is our sincerest prayer.

II. John Adams to James Warren,
Philadelphia, July 24, 1775

No doubt you've seen the last petition.
A certain piddling genius has just cast
All our doings in a silly light.
We're stuck between the Hawk and Buzzard.
By now we should have made a constitution,
Trained an army, and arrested all
Loyalists to be held as hostages
For all the dead in Boston.
Only then might they have sent the king
Petitions and addresses
And so on, blah blah blah.
Is this extravagant or wild?
Is it not the soundest policy?
Seven thousand pounds of powder came last night.
We'll send it soon as possible.
You must be patient.

Declaration of the Causes and Necessity of Taking up Arms

Congress, Philadelphia, July 6, 1775

A solemn reverence for the great Creator
Reveals to any man, the aim of government.
But long ago the British Parliament
Abandoned the promotion of its subjects'
Welfare, in a blind lust for limitless
Power. If they abjure the call to show
The larger world the reason of their acts,
We still esteem ourselves obliged to prove
The justice of our cause. Enumerations
Of all the injuries that we have suffered
Are legion, but sufficient case is made
By statutes that declare that Parliament
May bind us "in all cases whatsoever."
For ten years, with modest supplication,
We have besieged the throne—without effect.
Now, in Boston, martial law is exercised,
And General Gage says all the town's inhabitants
Are traitors. He exerts his utmost power
In spreading devastation and destruction.
Our choice has thus become submission, or
Resistance by armed force. We choose to fight.

His Majesty's Most Gracious Speech to Parliament

King George III, October 27, 1775

Lords, and Gentlemen:
Gross misrepresentations have inflamed
The colonies; and now their desperate leaders
Engage in open and avowed rebellion.
While many still retain their loyalty,
Too wise to miss the fatal consequence
Of usurpation, violence has compelled
Their meek submission. Wisdom recommends
Decisive acts, to bring a speedy end
To these disorders. When the multitude
Against whom all Our forces are directed
Abandon their delusion, We will receive
Them home, with mercy and with tenderness.
And still the earnest wishes of Our heart
Tend wholly to the safety and the happiness
Of all Our people; and the restoration
Of proper order and tranquility
Throughout the several parts of Our dominion.

Common Sense: Addressed to the Inhabitants of America

Thomas Paine, Philadelphia, January 1776

In these pages I offer nothing more
Than simple facts, plain arguments, and common sense.
The struggle for America has now
Become a test of arms; all plans proposed
Before last April are but almanacs
Of years gone by; and reconciliation
Has passed away like an agreeable
Dream. Britain is no mother country. Even brutes
Do not devour their young, nor savages
Make war upon their families. No one
Again can love or serve a power that
Brought fire and sword into his land; no more
Can you forgive the murders of Great Britain
Than can a man forgive the ravisher
Of his wife. Hark and listen, hear the dark
Blood of the slain cry out: *'tis time to part.*
O ye that love mankind, who dare oppose
Tyranny, stand forth! Freedom hath been hunted
Round the globe—Europe regards her like
A stranger—England warns her to depart.
O! Receive the fugitive, prepare
This new world an asylum for mankind.

Coda

General Orders: July 9, 1776

George Washington, Headquarters, New York City

Our Honorable Congress, impelled by twin
Dictates of duty and necessity,
Has seen fit to dissolve the bonds which once
Constrained this Country to Great Britain. It now
Declares the Colonies of North America
Free, and Independent States. This evening
All brigades are to be drawn on their
Parades, and there the new-passed Declaration
Showing the grounds and reasons of this measure
Shall be read for all to hear. This fresh
Incentive to Fidelity and Courage
Rewards us all with new realities:
The future peace and safety of this land
Depends alone on our success in arms;
That we are now in service of a State
Possessed of powers to reward our merit
And elevate us to those honored heights
So worthy of a people joined in freedom.

About the Author

Bradford Skow is a poet and a Professor of Philosophy at the Massachusetts Institute of Technology. He is the author of *Objective Becoming*; *Reasons Why*; and *Causation, Explanation, and the Metaphysics of Aspect*, all published by Oxford University Press. His newsletter *Mostly Aesthetics*, on poetry, philosophy, and the arts, may be found at mostlyaesthetics.com. This is his first book of poetry.